FIRST PEOPLES

THE MAORI
OF NEW ZEALAND

STEVE THEUNISSEN

Lerner Publications Company • Minneapolis

**First American edition published in 2003
by Lerner Publications Company**

Copyright © 2003 by Times Media Private Limited

Lerner Publications Company
A division of Lerner Publishing Group
241 First Avenue North
Minneapolis, MN 55401 U.S.A.
Website address: www.lernerbooks.com

Series originated and designed by
Times Editions
An imprint of Times Media Private Limited
A member of the Times Publishing Group
1 New Industrial Road, Singapore 536196
Website address: www.timesone.com.sg/te

Series editors: Margaret J. Goldstein, Paul Rozario
Series designers: Tuck Loong, Geoslyn Lim
Series picture researcher: Susan Jane Manuel

Published by arrangement with Times Editions

Library of Congress Cataloging-in-Publication Data
Theunissen, Steve.
The Maori of New Zealand / by Steve Theunissen.
p. cm. — (First peoples)
Includes bibliographical references and index.
Summary: An introduction to the history, modern and traditional cultural
practices, and economy of the Maori people of New Zealand.
ISBN 0-8225-0665-3 (lib. bdg. : alk. paper)
1. Maori (New Zealand people)—Juvenile literature.
[1. Maori (New Zealand people)] I. Title. II. Series.
CVeN   DU423.A1 T48 2003
993'.00499442—dc21   2002005525

Printed in Malaysia
Bound in the United States of America

1 2 3 4 5 6—0S—08 07 06 05 04 03

CONTENTS

WHO ARE THE MAORI?

The Maori are the original inhabitants of New Zealand, a small island country located far south in the Pacific Ocean. The Maori came to New Zealand as long as 1,500 years ago. They traveled in canoes from Tahiti, the Cook Islands, and other Pacific islands. The people of the south and central Pacific islands are known as Polynesians.

The Modern Maori

The Maori number about 500,000 people, or about 15 percent of the population of New Zealand (*left*). More than three-quarters of Maori live in New Zealand's large towns and cities. About 20,000 Maori live in the nearby country of Australia. Maori hold jobs in all areas of the workforce and share fully in the modern New Zealand lifestyle. Very few Maori live the traditional lifestyle of their ancestors. Recent decades, however, have seen a revival of interest in Maori culture. Many Maori are learning to treasure their culture. They want to keep it alive for future generations.

GROUPS AND SUBGROUPS

The Maori (*right*) refer to themselves as the Tangata Whenua, which means "people of the land." The Maori are divided into many different tribes, called *iwis*. Each iwi has its own dialect, or variation on the Maori language. Each iwi has its own way of doing things. Iwis are split into several *hapus*, or subtribes. The *whanau* is an even smaller division, consisting of an extended family.

LAND AT THE BOTTOM OF THE WORLD

New Zealand covers an area of 103,710 square miles (268,680 square kilometers). It contains two main islands: the North Island and the South Island. The islands hold a wide range of beautiful landscapes, including long sandy beaches, snowcapped mountains, and volcanoes.

Above: Sheep graze on the Canterbury Plains on the South Island.

Diverse Landscapes

The islands that became New Zealand were once part of a great southern continent called Gondwanaland. Over millions of years, this continent began to break up and drift apart. It eventually became many separate landmasses, including present-day Australia, Antarctica, and New Zealand.

Below: The Southern Alps are mountains on the South Island.

The North Island

About three-quarters of New Zealand's people live on the North Island. Auckland, the largest city in New Zealand, is located in the northern part of the North Island. Fertile farmlands lie south of Auckland in the Waikato River basin. The eastern coast of the island is home to dense forests, orchards, and vineyards. In the middle of the North Island lies the beautiful Bay of Plenty region. It boasts clear lakes and geothermal features such as hot springs and geysers. The North Island's most southern city is Wellington, the capital of New Zealand.

The South Island

The South Island is the larger of New Zealand's two main islands. On the island's east coast, the Canterbury Plains contain fertile farmland. In the northern part of the island, fertile soil and a good year-round climate provide the ideal environment for growing grapes to be made into wine. The island also features eight national parks. The South Island is often called "the Jewel of New Zealand" because of its stunning scenery. The island holds the snowcapped Southern Alps, clear lakes surrounded by towering mountains, unspoiled native forests, and sunny beaches. It has breathtaking fjords—deep, narrow bays that cut into the coastline, often with mountains rising up on each side. It also has slow-moving ice sheets called glaciers.

FISHED UP FROM THE SEA

Maori legend tells how New Zealand was created. The story says that Maui, a great fisherman from the legendary island of Hawaiki, set out on a deep-sea fishing voyage. He fished up a giant island from the sea. The island was too big to bring home, so he left it floating in the ocean. Generations later, an adventurer named Kupe set out to find the island. After traveling for three days, Kupe and his crew came across a land covered with mist and clouds. It was the North Island (*above*).

GEOTHERMAL ACTION

Above: Minerals give this lake on the North Island its blue-green color.

New Zealand is full of geothermal activity. The word *geothermal* means "earth heat." It refers to heat energy from the inner core of the earth. Magma, hot molten rock at the center of the earth, can reach temperatures of 12,632 degrees Fahrenheit (7,000 degrees Celsius).

Hot Springs and Geysers

When underground water comes close to magma, the water boils. Steam and hot water sometimes escape upward through cracks in the earth, creating hot springs at the earth's surface. Some hot springs throw up jets of hot water and steam. These springs are called geysers. Hot springs and geysers are found throughout New Zealand. The Maori once used hot springs in their daily lives, for activities such as bathing, washing clothes, and heating their homes.

Explosive Mountains

Sometimes magma itself bursts up through openings in the earth's surface. These openings are called volcanoes. Most volcanoes take the form of mountains. New Zealand's North Island contains several active volcanoes. Mount Ruapehu is the highest mountain on the North Island. It erupted as recently as 1996. Mount Ngauruhoe is New Zealand's most active volcano. It has erupted sixty-one times since 1839.

Above: Mount Ngauruhoe rises majestically from the Tongariro National Park on the North Island.

Left: A geyser erupts from hot springs in Rotorua, North Island.

A Volcanic Island

Sitting about 30 miles (48.3 kilometers) off the North Island's east coast, White Island is actually a volcanic mountain. It is the largest volcano in New Zealand, but 70 percent of it is underwater.

GEOTHERMAL POWER

New Zealand has seven geothermal power stations. The stations (*left*) use steam escaping from the earth to produce electricity. Geothermal energy provides around 13.5 percent of New Zealand's power. Geothermal power is inexpensive and renewable—the earth provides an endless supply of energy for free. But the process of changing geothermal energy into electricity can hurt the environment. The process produces extreme heat and chemical wastes, which can kill fish and other wildlife.

THE PLANTS OF NEW ZEALAND

Many types of plants and trees grow in New Zealand. About 80 percent of them are endemic to New Zealand, meaning they are found nowhere else on earth. The country has many national parks that help preserve and protect much of this plant life.

Forest Lands

Forests cover about 25 percent of New Zealand's land area. Beech forests are the most common. These forests feature five different kinds of beech trees. Shrubs grow beneath the trees, and the forest floor is carpeted with ferns. Kauri forests, dominated by the massive kauri tree, are mainly found on the western side of the North Island. Pohutukawa trees grow along the rocky western coast of the North Island.

Below: Luxuriant forests on the North Island

Ferns Galore

More than 150 types of ferns grow in New Zealand. In fact, the fern leaf is one of New Zealand's national emblems. One of the most common ferns is the bracken fern. It was once a source of food for the Maori, who loved to chew on its stem.

Left: Exotic fern forests house many species of indigenous animals and insects.

Conserving Nature

Almost 300 kinds of plants and animals in New Zealand are in danger of extinction. Pollution, the logging of native forests, and the spread of towns and cities have destroyed many wilderness areas. Pests such as opossums, rats, wild pigs, and wild cats have also destroyed plant life in many areas. In recent decades, New Zealand has begun many programs to protect wilderness areas and endangered species.

Above: Kauri trees are tall and have extremely large trunks.

PLANTS FOR MEDICINE

The Maori people have long known about the healing properties of certain native plants and flowers (*right*). Karamu is a shrub that can relieve stomach and urinary problems. Koromiko, a plant found growing in gravel and along creek beds on the South Island, cures diarrhea and dysentery.

NEW ZEALAND WILDLIFE

Above: The unusual tuatara lizard

The first Polynesians to arrive in New Zealand brought dogs, rats, pigs, and a kind of chicken called the moa. The pig and the moa could not adjust to the weather in New Zealand, which is colder than most other Pacific islands. These animals did not survive. But the Maori found a tall, flightless bird in their new home. They named this bird moa, after the chickens that had perished in the cold. The Maori soon hunted the moa to extinction.

A Land of Birds

Modern New Zealand is home to hundreds of different types of birds. Some of them, such as the kiwi and the weka, are unable to fly. The kea, a type of large parrot, lives high in the mountains. The tui has dark glossy feathers and pure white feathery tufts at the throat. Oceanic birds, such as the albatross and the petrel, are numerous in New Zealand. Shorebirds like the dotterel are also common.

Right: A playful kea

Millions of Sheep

European setters, arriving in the mid-1850s, brought sheep to New Zealand. The New Zealand Romney is the most common kind of sheep in New Zealand. It makes up around 60 percent of the sheep population. First introduced to New Zealand in 1858, the Romney provides good wool for making carpets. Merino sheep are also highly prized for their wool.

Below: New Zealand has more sheep than people.

Insects and Reptiles

New Zealand is home to a number of interesting reptiles and insects. A lizard called the tuatara is a relative of the extinct dinosaurs. Tuataras can live to be seventy years old. The weta, a type of grasshopper, is New Zealand's largest insect. Wetas can measure up to 4.5 inches (11 centimeters) in length. They are often found in gardens, woodsheds, and basements. About 2,000 species of spiders live in New Zealand.

The only poisonous type is the katipo, which lives under rocks and around sandy beaches.

THE NEW ZEALAND ICON

The shy kiwi (*below*), one of New Zealand's national symbols, is a flightless bird. It has whiskers like a cat and shaggy feathers that look like fur. It burrows in the ground like a mole. The kiwi also has a long beak, which it uses to probe in the ground for food.

THE GREAT MIGRATIONS

Travelers from other Pacific islands first reached New Zealand as early as 1,500 years ago. Historians are not sure why they came to New Zealand. Their home islands might have become overpopulated, or food might have run short, causing the people to look for a new home. Maori legend says the first Maori set out from the island of Hawaiki in a fleet of seven canoes. It is said that all Maori people can trace their origins back to travelers in these canoes.

Surviving the Voyage

These first New Zealanders were expert sailors. They traveled across the vast waters of the South Pacific Ocean in fleets of double-hulled canoes—two canoes connected by a platform. Each canoe could carry up to thirty-five people. It had sails woven from coconut leaves. The travelers navigated by the stars. To survive, they carried provisions of dried and salted fish; fresh pig, dog, and chicken meat; coconuts and other kinds of fruit; and roots such as sweet potatoes.

Below: This engraving from the 1700s depicts a Maori war canoe.

Above: Some historians believe the Maori came from Easter Island in the South Pacific Ocean.

A Different Land

The early Maori settled on the northeast coast of the North Island. As more canoes arrived, people began to settle on other parts of the North Island and on the South Island. The newcomers faced hardships in their new land. They had come from warm, tropical islands. In New Zealand, the sea was cold. The weather changed dramatically with the seasons. The foods people had grown on their home islands—kava, coconut, and bananas—would not grow in New Zealand.

THE HOME ISLANDS

The ancestors of the Maori probably came from Tahiti, the Society Islands, Easter Island, Hawaii, and the Cook Islands. These islanders survived by fishing in the warm waters of coral reefs and sheltered lagoons. They ate fruits such as bananas, coconuts, and breadfruit. The islanders were very spiritual. They worshipped the natural elements: the earth, sky, and sea.

A NEW WORLD

In New Zealand, the Maori settlers found many natural resources to help them in daily life. They found wood that was excellent for building houses. They used flax plants and bird feathers to make clothing. They made knives from obsidian, a dark volcanic glass. The Maori soon learned the habits of New Zealand's birds and fishes, which they killed for food. They learned which berries were safe to eat and which ones were poisonous. They developed a twelve-month calendar, which helped them grow crops according to the seasons.

Below: This illustration shows the courtyard of a traditional Maori settlement.

Conquering the Interior

For the first few hundred years of settlement, Maori people lived around the top and bottom of the North Island and along the coasts of the South Island. These areas were easy to reach by canoe. They had large populations of moas and seals, which the Maori hunted for food. Eventually, all the moas along the coast were killed. Hunters had to travel farther inland to find more of these big birds. People began to settle in New Zealand's interior.

Right: A Maori chief from the 1700s

From Hunting to Farming

By the 1600s, the Maori had developed a complex society, with its own religion, laws, and leaders. Different tribes inhabited different regions. Tribes sometimes warred with one another. By then, the moa had almost been hunted to extinction. Seals had also been killed in great numbers. People began to turn to farming as a way to get food.

DEATH OF THE MOA

What we know about the moa comes from the many skeletons and fossils found throughout New Zealand. These remains reveal that the largest moa stood about 10 feet (3 meters) tall. It had a small head, a blunt beak, powerful but short legs, no wings, and no tail. Because moas were so big, they needed a great deal of food. They ate twigs, berries, and other fruits. The Maori hunted moas with spears. By about 1700, the bird had been completely hunted out. This image of a moa (*left*) is a model.

EUROPEAN CONTACT

The first European to sail close to New Zealand was a Dutch adventurer named Abel Tasman. Tasman reached the North Island in December 1642. But he sailed away after a violent dispute with some Maori onboard his ship. In 1769 English explorer James Cook reached New Zealand. The first European settlers soon followed.

Righ: A statue of Captain James Cook

White Settlers

The first European settlers were sealers. They set up camps along the South Island coast in the 1790s. The Maori called the Europeans Pakehas. Most of the settlers were British. They brought new tools, animals, and crops to New Zealand. They also brought diseases that the Maori had never known before. Tuberculosis, venereal disease, measles, and influenza spread rapidly through Maori villages. These diseases caused a 50 percent decline in the Maori population between 1820 and 1920.

Below: Maori chiefs pose in their traditional clothes in this illustration from the 1800s.

The Treaty of Waitangi

More and more British settlers arrived in New Zealand. They bought land from the Maori for almost nothing. The idea of selling land was foreign to the Maori. They believed that the settlers were just borrowing the land. In 1840 the British government signed the Treaty of Waitangi with forty-five Maori chiefs. Under the treaty, the Maori gave New Zealand to the British Empire. In return, the Maori were guaranteed rights to their land and were given the rights and privileges of British citizens.

Right: This watercolor painting from the mid-1800s shows Maori warriors performing a war dance.

The Land Wars

But the British did not honor the treaty. In the 1840s and 1850s, the British government forced the Maori to sell more and more land. Fights sometimes broke out between Maori and white settlers. In the mid-1840s, Maori chiefs Hone Heke and Kawiti led a rebellion against the British in the upper North Island. They won some spectacular victories before they were defeated. Wars raged on through the 1870s. Eventually, the British defeated the Maori.

PUKETAKAUERE

Wiremu Kingi was a strong Maori chief. He gathered more than 1,000 Maori from all over the North Island to face about 3,500 British troops. In 1860, his army defeated the British at the village of Puketakauere. The battle has been called one of the most clear-cut and disastrous defeats suffered by British troops in New Zealand. This 1887 illustration (*left*) shows Chief Rangihuatau with his *mere*, a greenstone club used in battle.

TWENTIETH-CENTURY CHANGES

B y the beginning of the 1900s, the Maori population had fallen from about 200,000 to just 42,000. The average life span for a Maori was just twenty-eight years for a woman and twenty-four years for a man. The Maori suffered from disease, unsanitary living conditions, impure water, and poor health care. Many New Zealanders, Maoris and whites alike, felt something needed to be done to improve Maori life.

Above: The 1911 coat of arms of the Dominion of New Zealand

The Young Maori Party

In 1897, students at Te Aute College, a school for young Maori men, met to discuss ways to help the Maori people. Over time, this group evolved into an organization called the Young Maori Party. The group wanted to improve life for the Maori in areas such as housing, health care, education, and employment. Some remarkable leaders emerged from the Young Maori Party. Apirana Ngata served in New Zealand's parliament. Maui Pomare was a doctor who led a national program to improve the health of Maori people.

Left: Many Maori played for the New Zealand Rugby Union Football team in the early 1900s.

Leaving the Land

Life improved for the Maori after World War II. Because of the work of Maui Pomare and other leaders, Maori began to receive better health care. The Maori population began to grow rapidly. Many Maori people moved from rural areas to cities after the war, mainly in search of work.

Left: Students at Te Aute College. *Right:* A Maori man waves the Maori flag.

The Protest Years

When Maori moved to the cities, they often lost touch with their cultural and family heritage. Many young Maori were no longer aware of Maori legends and traditions. Fewer Maori spoke the Maori language. The Maori also suffered from social problems, including unemployment and poverty. In the 1970s, groups of Maori organized sit-ins and demonstrations. They wanted to bring Maori problems to public attention and to protest the loss of the traditional Maori way of life.

The Waitangi Tribunal

In 1975 the New Zealand government formed a commission called the Waitangi Tribunal. This 16-member group, made up of whites and Maoris, allows the Maori to make claims when they believe that the 1840 Treaty of Waitangi has been violated. For instance, in 1982 the Te Ati Awa tribe challenged the right of a petrochemical company to discharge waste into coastal waters near the tribe's homeland. The tribunal found that the coastal reefs and shellfish belong to the Maori people. As such, they are protected under the Treaty of Waitangi.

FIGHTING FOR THEIR COUNTRY

When New Zealand entered World War I, young Maori men were quick to join the military. Many of them served in the Pioneer Battalion, an all-Maori force that left for Europe in 1915. Over the next three years, these soldiers earned high regard as courageous fighting men. Later, more than 17,000 Maori enlisted to fight in World War II. Many served with the famous 28th Maori Battalion. They earned distinction as brave fighters on the battlefields of Europe. This tombstone (*left*) marks the grave of a Maori soldier who fought and died in World War I.

THE TRADING ECONOMY

Above: A European whaling ship in the 1800s

Before the arrival of Europeans, the Maori had no form of money. People in different villages bartered, or traded, for the items they needed. Maori from coastal areas would often travel inland to exchange foods like dried shark and other ocean fish for freshwater fish. Other valuable trade items included obsidian and greenstone, a semiprecious stone.

European Trade

The arrival of Europeans in the late 1700s changed the Maori economy. The first European sailors brought many new goods to the Maori, including iron gardening tools; fruit trees; and crops like wheat, corn, and potatoes. In exchange for these items, the Maori gave the Europeans timber, flax, woven goods, and carvings. By the 1830s, some Europeans were working as middlemen between white and Maori traders. These men were called Pakeha-Maori. They normally married Maori women and lived in Maori villages.

Below: A colored woodcut shows the town of Dunedin, South Island, in 1860.

Above: The introduction of the railway in New Zealand helped the country's economic growth in the late 1800s.

From Trade to Warfare

White settlers established farms and ranches across New Zealand. They were hungry for more and more land. In the late 1800s, disputes over land erupted into warfare between Maoris and whites. When war broke out, the trading economy between the Maori and the whites collapsed.

EUROPEAN TRADE

European trade was very damaging to Maori society. For example, white traders introduced guns to the Maori, which led to increased warfare between tribes. Alcohol, another European trade item, created social problems within Maori villages. White traders also brought blankets that carried deadly diseases to Maori villages. Finally, European trade introduced the Maori to the idea of money and individual owner-ship. Previously, the Maori had shared possessions with one another. The decline in community sharing weakened Maori society. This photograph (*right*) shows a barrel and harpoon from a whaling ship of the 1800s.

THE MODERN ECONOMY

Most modern Maori live a typical urban lifestyle. Maori work in all sectors of the New Zealand economy. Many hold factory or construction jobs, but others work as politicians, lawyers, doctors, teachers, athletes, actors, police officers, and scientists. The Maori still struggle with poverty, however. Maori people are three times more likely than non-Maori to be unemployed. The average Maori family earns $10,000 less per year than the average non-Maori family.

Closing the Gaps

The New Zealand government has introduced a range of programs to help Maori people achieve the same living standards as non-Maori. These efforts are called the Closing the Gaps program. The government has also helped Maori people start businesses in areas such as tourism, fishing, and dairy farming.

Left: A Maori fisherman proudly displays his catch for the day.

New Businesses

In many cases, the Waitangi Tribunal has required the New Zealand government to pay Maori tribes for land that was taken from them unfairly. As a result of these payments, many tribes have large sums of money to invest. Some tribes have started new Maori-owned businesses, especially in the areas of agriculture, horticulture, and tourism. These businesses provide jobs for thousands of Maori.

Left: A bustling street in Wellington, North Island

The Tourist Trade

Many Maori work in the tourism industry, and tourists in New Zealand are eager to learn about Maori culture. The city of Rotorua, in the middle of the North Island, is popular with tourists. Visitors there can enjoy Maori concerts, visit traditional Maori villages, and feast on Maori foods. Rotorua also has many geothermal wonders, such as geysers, boiling mud pools, and hot waterfalls.

WHAKAREWAREWA THERMAL VILLAGE

At Whakarewarewa Village in Rotorua, Maori people live just as their ancestors did hundreds of years ago. Guided tours allow visitors to see how the Maori once cooked food, wove, and carved unique designs. Visitors (*right*) also see how the Maori used geothermal features such as hot springs for bathing and heating in winter. Maori performers give twice-daily concerts of traditional song and dance at the village.

TRADITIONAL HOMES

Above: Semipermanent traditional Maori homes

The vast majority of Maori live in modern-style houses in the city. In rural areas, however, a few groups still live like their ancestors did. They live in wooden houses surrounding a communal meetinghouse. These structures are similar to the dwellings of the early Maori settlers.

Evolving Homes

Below: A beautiful Maori meetinghouse in Rotorua, North Island

When the Maori first arrived in New Zealand, they moved frequently to follow the moa flocks. Because they moved often, they did not build elaborate homes. They built simple huts consisting of circular wooden frames covered with palm leaves and grasses. Eventually, starting around the 1500s, moas became scarce. The Maori traveled less and less. They eventually became farmers and built permanent settlements, including elaborate wooden houses shaped like upturned boats.

The Whare Puni

The *whare puni*, or sleeping house, was a rectangular building with sunken floors and walls about 4 feet (1.2 meters) high. Doors and windows were made as small as possible and fitted with sliding covers to keep in warmth. The whare puni housed a whanau, or extended family, which could include up to two dozen people. A fireplace inside warmed the home. People slept on mats woven from ferns and flax.

Above: This watercolor shows a more permanent Maori home.

Storage and Cooking Houses

Dried fish and other foods were kept in a storehouse, carved with beautiful decorations. The house was built on raised poles as protection from rats. Another storehouse held highly prized tools, weapons, feathered cloaks, and food offerings for the gods. Food was prepared in a separate structure, or outside in an underground oven.

Right: A traditional Maori storehouse designed to keep meat

THE MEETINGHOUSE

The *whare whakairo*, or meetinghouse, was the central building in the village. People gathered there on winter nights and recounted the legends and history of their tribe. The building was a large rectangular room with a large porch out front. Every piece of interior timber was intricately carved with images of ancestors or was painted with spiral designs.

THE KAINGA AND THE PA

The first Maori villages were called *kaingas*. The typical kainga was home to several whanaus, for a total population of about fifty people. The kainga was surrounded by a fence, with a garden beyond. These early villages had no defensive walls or ditches.

Above: An illustration of a Maori storehouse from the late 1700s

Below: A colored woodcut shows life in a typical Maori village of the mid-1800s.

The Village Garden

The villagers grew mostly *kumaras*, a kind of sweet potato, in their gardens. Other food crops included fern roots and cabbage trees. The ground was carefully prepared with digging sticks. Sand and ashes were added to the soil to make it more fertile.

Right: With its reconstructed traditional Maori buildings, the Tamaki Village in Rotorua, North Island, gives visitors a glimpse into Maori life before Europeans arrived in New Zealand.

Fortified Villages

Over time, enemies began to raid kainga gardens. So people began to build fortified villages, called *pas*. A hilltop, ridge top, or cliff was a good site for a pa, since the site could be easily defended. Villagers built ditches, terraces, and stockades around pas for defense. The inside of the pa was divided into small walled-off sections, which meant that attackers—if they managed to get inside the pa—had to fight for each section.

THE MARAE

In front of the village meetinghouse was an open courtyard called a *marae*. Tribal meetings were held there. Visitors were welcomed there with special greetings and speeches, which related tribal history and legend. Visitors would then be entertained with songs and chants. The marae was a highly spiritual place for the Maori. People began meetings there with a prayer to the spirits, asking for protection.

TRADITIONAL MAORI SOCIETY

In Maori creation myths, men were said to be the children of the god Tane. That made men *tapu,* or sacred. Since men were sacred, they could not carry anything on their backs. Women had to carry heavy loads. Men could work only on sacred projects, such as building canoes and planting crops. Men were also the carvers and fishermen of the village. Maori women tended the gardens, gathered wild plants, cooked, and collected firewood and shellfish. Women descended from chiefs were the village weavers.

Social Divisions

Maori tribes were divided into several social classes. The most important person was the high chief. He traced his ancestry directly from the gods. Then came the chief's immediate family and others who had achieved high rank through their accomplishments. The priest was next in rank. He determined which people and places were sacred. He was also responsible for remembering and telling the tribe's history. Skilled artists and warriors were the next class. They were followed by the common people—the ones who worked the land and cooked the food. The lowest in rank were slaves captured from other tribes.

Right: Elderly Maori gather at a meetinghouse in Gisborne, North Island.

Facing page, bottom: A Maori couple rubs noses together. This is the traditional Maori way of greeting people.

Below: An illustration of a Maori family in the early 1800s

Private Property

Most items within the village belonged to everyone who lived there. A man had a few private possessions, however, including a greenstone mere, or fighting club, and a fishhook. A woman might possess a special piece of clothing, some handmade jewelry, a stone used to prepare food, and a pair of carved sticks used for weaving.

THE MAORI WARRIOR

Warfare between Maori tribes was not common during the moa-hunting period. When food became harder to get, however, tribes fought more frequently over land and resources. By the time he reached manhood, the Maori warrior (*right*) was skilled in the use of many weapons. Spears were used mainly for defense. The *taiaha* was a paddle-shaped club used for close fighting. The greenstone mere had a thin edge that could cause much damage to an enemy. When facing the enemy just before a battle, Maori warriors would shout loudly and stick their tongues out in order to scare the enemy.

CHANGING TRADITIONS

Modern Maori are fully integrated into New Zealand society. The vast majority of Maori live in cities. Yet ties to home villages remain strong. Urban Maori often return to their tribal lands for funerals, weddings, and family reunions. There, they embrace the traditions of old.

Maori in Government

Maori society is no longer governed by chiefs. Instead, modern Maori participate in all levels of New Zealand government. Five seats in the nation's parliament are reserved for Maori representatives, but Maori actually hold many more seats. In fact, Maori representatives make up about 20 percent of the 120-member parliament. When it comes to tribal issues, Maori elders are the spokespeople for their communities.

New Leaders

A number of Maori have emerged from the academic world and the Maori protest movement. Whina Cooper was a leader in the movement for Maori rights. In the 1950s, she founded the Maori Women's Welfare League, a group that worked to improve life for Maori women. Another leader is Ranginui Walker, a professor of Maori studies at the University of Auckland.

Cultural Revival

The 1990s saw a huge revival of interest in Maori culture, especially among young Maori. Schools began to teach the Maori language. It also joined English as an official language of New Zealand. A new generation of Maori embraced traditional Maori arts such as carving and weaving. Internationally acclaimed Maori writers, including Witi Ihimaera, Alan Duff, and Keri Hulme, described Maori culture in books. Maori television shows also contributed to the revival of Maori culture.

Above: A Maori family sits down to dinner in Rotorua, North Island.

Right: Maori sisters smile for the camera in South Island.

TE MAORI

The *Te Maori* exhibition opened at the Metropolitan Museum of Art in New York in 1984, before touring several other U.S. cities. The exhibition featured ancient Maori artifacts, along with the performance of Maori rituals and ceremonies. Many thousands of Americans visited the exhibit and experienced the vibrant, living culture of the Maori. On returning to New Zealand, *Te Maori* was shown in major cities, where it was received enthusiastically.

Left: The "Beehive" in Wellington, North Island, is the home of New Zealand's parliament.

DRESS AND DECORATION

Above: An intricate Maori skirt made from grass

Modern Maori wear western-style clothing, similar to styles worn in Europe and the United States. Maori wear traditional outfits only on special occasions. But these clothes are still a very important part of Maori culture. Some modern fashion designers even use Maori images and patterns in their clothing.

Men's Attire

For working or fighting, Maori men wore only a breechcloth at the waist. For formal occasions, men wore various kinds of cloaks and capes. One kind of cloak was made from flax fiber, decorated with strips of dog skin and hair. Men also wore ornaments around their necks and feathers or greenstone earrings in their ears. Men typically wore their hair in a topknot. They usually dyed their bodies with a red dye made from ocher, a kind of iron.

Women's Wear

For Maori women, everyday dress consisted of a girdle of braided flax cord around the waist, with a fringe of leaves in front. Women also wore skirts made from strands of dyed flax. On formal occasions, women wore beautifully decorated capes made of flax fiber or dog skin.

Left: An illustration of a Maori girl of the early 1800s. She wears a cloak made of flax and carries flax in her hand.

Right: Bushes of flax growing in New Zealand's countryside

The Wonders of Flax

More than sixty varieties of flax grow in New Zealand. The long, green leaves of the plant contain strong white fiber. The Maori used the fiber to make warm clothing. European settlers used the fiber to make rope. The Maori often traded flax with Europeans. The Maori also used flax for medicine. Flax oil was used to heal wounds.

THE MAORI TATTOO

Both Maori men and women wore *moko,* or face tattoos (*right*). Women tattooed only their chins and lips. Warriors tattooed their entire faces, as well as their buttocks and thighs. Moko was applied when a young person reached the age of marriage. It announced that he or she was available to the opposite sex. Spirals and curves were the most popular moko designs. The markings were made with dye, carved into the skin with small chisels made of bird bones. Some modern Maori still practice traditional tattooing.

Left: Maori women from the early 1900s wear a combination of grass skirts and European-style blouses.

THE ART OF THE MAORI

The Maori have always been an artistic people. Warriors decorated their faces with swirled tattoos. Other traditional arts included carving and weaving.

Left: An intricately carved wooden Maori flute

Below: A Maori woman embroiders traditional Maori patterns onto a cloak.

Maori Weaving

Maori women used flax to weave sandals, skirts, cloaks, baskets, and mats. They decorated their weavings with dyes made from berries, as well as with feathers and dog hair. Women also wove wall coverings, which were decorated with diamonds and other symmetrical shapes. Modern artists still practice traditional Maori weaving arts.

The Carving Tradition

The first Maori in New Zealand found high-quality timber for building their homes. The wood of the totara tree was especially easy to split and work with stone tools. Men carved designs into the logs used to make walls, doors, and pillars. The most popular image was the human form, with a realistic face with complex tattoo markings but an out-of-proportion body—too small and squat. Scary-looking figures with tongues poking out were placed at the entrances to Maori fortresses to frighten enemies. Modern Maori carvers have kept the old traditions alive. Maori carvings are popular with tourists.

Above: A Maori woodcarver on the South Island skillfully carves a wooden Maori sculpture.

THE WONDROUS POUNAMU

In the 1600s, the Maori found a beautiful type of greenstone on New Zealand's South Island. They called it *pounamu*. It became their most prized carving stone, used to make delicate jewelry (*right*) as well as clubs for fighting. Items made from pounamu were highly prized and were handed down from one generation to the next.

A SONG FOR EVERY OCCASION

The love of song is common among Polynesian peoples. For the Maori, singing is a way of expressing feelings, as well as a way to pass on history and myths. The Maori had songs for every occasion—love songs, chants and prayers to the gods, songs to welcome visitors onto a marae. Some songs were thought to have a spiritual and mystical force.

Below: Maoris perform an action song in Rotorua, North Island.

Song and Dance

Dancing and singing were inseparable in traditional Maori culture. Villagers gathered to sing and dance in the evenings. On important occasions, such as the welcoming of visitors from another tribe, the village's best performers would dress in their finest clothing and ornaments to dance and sing. Both men and women performed. Those who excelled were greatly admired.

Left: Dame Kiri Te Kanawa is one of the world's most famous sopranos. She has Maori roots.

Right: A Maori dancer performs traditional action songs.

Action Songs

Hakas were Maori action songs. Singers used their hands, feet, legs, bodies, tongues, and even eyes to help impart the song's message. The Maori had many different types of hakas, each with its own purpose and style. The haka maimai, for example, was performed during the period of mourning for the dead. The haka pirori was performed to avenge an injury or insult. It was accompanied by actions that showed contempt for the watchers.

KA MATE—HAKA OF THE ALL BLACKS

The New Zealand national rugby team—the All Blacks (*left*)—has been performing the Ka Mate haka before its international games since 1905. The words were composed in 1820 by High Chief Te Rauparaha as he hid in a kumara pit from his enemies. The haka is performed as a challenge to the opposing team. It includes rhythmic thigh and chest beating and a concluding high leap.

THE LANGUAGE OF THE MAORI

The Maori language is part of the Polynesian family of languages. It is closely related to languages spoken in the Cook Islands, Tahiti, and Hawaii. The Maori language, along with English, is one of the national languages of New Zealand.

The Oral Tradition

The Maori have passed down stories, songs, myths, and legends from generation to generation over hundreds of years. The *tohunga*, or priest, was the main villager in charge of remembering and telling history. Many priests had amazing memories, especially when it came to remembering genealogies, or family trees.

Right: A Maori man speaks at a meetinghouse.

KO WIKITORIA TE KUINI O INOARANI
I TANA MAHARA ATAWAI KI NCA RANCA-
TIRA ME NCA HATU O NU-TIRAIH I TANA
HIAHIA·HOKI KIA TOHUNCIA KI A RATOU
O RATOU RANCATIRATANCA ME TO RATOU
WENHA AKIA MAU TOHU HOKI TE RONCO KI A
PATOU MC TE ATA NOHO HOKI KUA WA-
KAARO IA HE MEA TIKA KIA TUKUA MAI
TE TAHI RANCATIRA HEI KAI WAKARITE
KI NCA TANCATA MAORI O NU-TIRANI KIA
WAKAAETIA E NCA RANCATIRAMAORI TE
KAWANATANCA O TE KUINI KI NCA WAHI
KATOA O TE WENUA NEI ME NCA MOTU NA
TE MEA HOKI HE TOKOMAHA KE NOA
TANCATA O TONAIWI KUA NOHO KITENCI
WENUA A E HAERE MAI NEI.

Above: Part of the text of the Treaty of Waitangi written in the Maori language

The Written Language

Before Europeans came to New Zealand, Maori was an unwritten language. Storytelling and singing were the only ways to pass on history and legends. European missionaries, or religious teachers, were the first ones to write down the Maori language. They began to translate the Bible into Maori as early as 1814. English professor Samuel Lee came to New Zealand in the 1820s. He worked closely with several Maori chiefs to write down the language using the Roman alphabet.

Forbidden Language

In the 1880s, large numbers of Maori children began attending European-style schools. There, Maori students were punished for speaking their own language in class. In the early 1900s, many Maori parents encouraged their children to learn English instead of Maori. These parents thought that speaking English would help their children succeed in New Zealand society. Soon, the numbers of Maori who could speak their own language dropped dramatically.

Right: This statue honors Pania of the Reef, a figure in Maori legend.

Revival

In the mid-1980s, Maori leaders became increasingly aware of the risk of losing their language. They established five schools (called "language nests") to teach Maori to preschool children. The program was an immediate success. More than 800 similar schools were then opened around New Zealand. These centers are very important in keeping the Maori language alive.

INFORMATION TECHNOLOGY– MAORI STYLE

Electronic Reference Information, a company based in Christchurch, has combined new technology with ancient culture. The company's CD-ROM Maori dictionary is used by thousands of people to learn and teach the Maori language. The company also sells a Maori spellchecker.

PANIA
OF THE REEF

AN OLD MAORI LEGEND
TELLS HOW PANIA, LURED
BY THE SIREN VOICES OF
THE SEA PEOPLE, SWAM OUT
TO MEET THEM. WHEN SHE
ENDEAVOURED TO RETURN TO
HER LOVER, SHE WAS TRANS
-FORMED INTO THE REEF
WHICH NOW LIES BEYOND
THE NAPIER BREAKWATER.

TO PERPETUATE THE LEGEND
THE THIRTY THOUSAND CLUB
PRESENTED THIS STATUE TO
THE CITY OF NAPIER 1954.

THE MAORI SPIRIT WORLD

Religion played a role in every part of pre-European Maori life. Even the most routine tasks had to be carried out properly, according to religious beliefs. If not, the gods would be angered.

Right: The stained-glass panels of Saint Faith's Maori Church in Rotorua, North Island

Many Gods

The Maori were polytheistic, meaning that they worshipped many different gods. Tangaroa was the god of the sea. Tane was the god of forests and trees. Rangi was the god of the sky. Some gods were friendly, but all of them were capable of awesome displays of anger. Sickness, accidents, and death were all seen as signs that the spirits were unhappy.

Below: The baptism of Te Ngahue, an aged Maori chief, in 1849

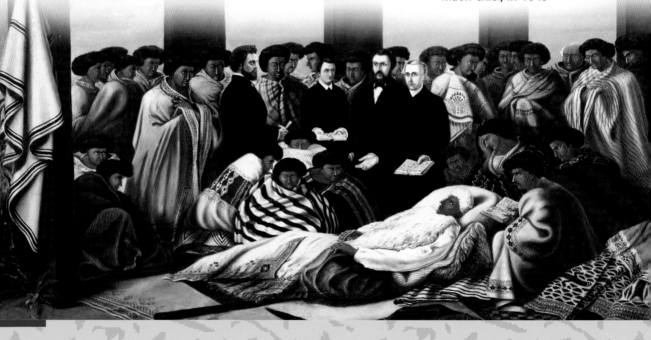

The Work of the Missionaries

The first English missionaries arrived in New Zealand in 1814. They wanted the Maori to practice Christianity instead of their traditional religion. At first, the Maori rejected Christianity. In the late 1820s, however, things began to change. Missionaries were seen as messengers of peace, providing a bridge between Maoris and Europeans. The missionaries also helped the Maori obtain medical treatment, food, and supplies from the Europeans. Because of the missionaries' goodwill, Maori soon converted to Christianity in great numbers.

Maori Prophets

In the late 1800s and early 1900s, several Maori prophets started new religious movements that mixed traditional and Christian beliefs. Horopapera Tuwhakararo began a movement called Pai Marire (Good and Peaceful) in 1862, after he dreamed of visitations by the Archangel Gabriel. Another prophet was Rua Kenana, born in 1868. He built a religious community at Maungapohatu. At its peak, it had over 1,000 members. T. W. Ratana, born in 1870, converted many Maori to his church. It is still a part of the religious landscape of New Zealand.

Above: A Maori preacher delivers a sermon from the pulpit of Saint Paul's Church, Auckland, North Island.

HOW THE EARTH CAME TO BE

In the beginning, according to Maori legend, the Sky Father (Rangi) and the Earth Mother (Papa) united and had many children. But the parents lay clasped so tightly together that the children were cramped in darkness. Six children plotted to make space in which to live and grow. One child suggested that they push Rangi away into the distance. This they did, thus creating the sky above the earth. Sometimes, Rangi weeps for Papa. His tears are raindrops.

FEASTS AND FESTIVALS

Festivals and ceremonies have always been a big part of Maori life. Some ceremonies were performed to please the gods and spirits. Others were held purely for entertainment. The Maori still hold festivals and ceremonies as a way to preserve their cultural traditions.

Kapa Haka

Many Maori belong to performing arts clubs called kapa hakas. There, members perform action songs, war dances, and other traditional dances, as well as the Maori women's traditional *karanga* call—a shrill, high-pitched call of welcome. Clubs compete against each other on the local, regional, and tribal levels.

Below: A Maori kapa haka performs a farewell song.

The Hangi

The highlight of many gatherings was the laying of the traditional Maori *hangi,* or feast. Using paper, wood, and stones, villagers built a fire in a large hole in the ground. When the stones were white hot, villagers poured water on them to produce steam. Food was then steam-cooked for several hours. Chicken, pork, potatoes, pumpkin, and kumara were favorite hangi ingredients.

Above: Traditional Maori delicacies that have been prepared for a Maori feast

A Special Celebration

In 1990, the Maori commemorated the 150th anniversary of the signing of the Treaty of Waitangi. As part of the celebration, participants built *waka tauas*—traditional war canoes. Originally, these canoes were 60 to 100 feet (18 to 30 meters) long and could hold thirty warriors. The modern-day canoe builders used the traditional construction process. They made the canoes from massive kauri logs fitted with elaborately carved stern and bow pieces. The canoes were launched in elaborate traditional ceremonies.

THE AOTEAROA TRADITIONAL PERFORMING ARTS FESTIVAL

Begun in 1972, the Aotearoa Traditional Performing Arts Festival is the biggest Maori event in New Zealand and the world's largest gathering of indigenous people. More than thirty-five kapa haka teams from throughout New Zealand and Australia compete for the national championship. In all, over 2,000 performers appear onstage at the festival, which is held every two years.

GLOSSARY

artifacts: practical human-made objects remaining from a certain time in history

dialect: a regional variation on a language

endemic: found only in a certain region or country

extended family: a large family group, including cousins, grandparents, aunts, and uncles

extinction: the total elimination of a specific type of plant or animal

fjord: a long narrow arm of the sea bordered by steep cliffs

fossils: remains or impressions of living thing from earlier eras, preserved in the earth's crust

genealogy: a list of one's ancestors

geothermal: relating to heat from inside the earth

geyser: a hot spring that sends up fountainlike jets of water and steam into the air at regular intervals

haka (HA-ka): a Maori action song

indigenous people: the original people of a certain region or country

iwi (EE-wee): the Maori word for "tribe"

kainga (KANG-guh): a Maori village

marae (muh-RY): the open courtyard in front of a Maori meetinghouse

missionaries: religious teachers who try to convert others to their faith

pa (PAH): a fortified Maori village

polytheistic: worshipping many gods

pounamu (poo-NAH-moo): greenstone

tapu (tuh-POO): the Maori word for "sacred"; the English word *taboo* is derived from *tapu*

volcano: an opening in the earth's surface that occasionally erupts with magma and gases from deep inside the earth. Many volcanoes take the shape of mountains.

whanau (WAH-now): the Maori term for an extended family

whare puni (WAH-ray POO-nee): a storehouse

whare whakairo (WAH-ray wah-KY-roh): the meetinghouse and central building in a Maori village

FINDING OUT MORE

Books

Beck, Katie, and Nancy R. Thatch. *The Moas*. Kansas City, MO: Landmark Editions, Inc., 1999.

Bishop, Gavin. *Maui and the Sun: A Maori Tale*. New York, NY: North South Books, 1996.

Gillespie, Carol Ann. *New Zealand*. Philadelphia, PA: Chelsea House Publishers, 2002.

MacDonald, Robert. *Maori*. New York, NY: Thomson Learning, 1994.

Ryan, Pat. *New Zealand*. Plymouth, MN: Child's World, 1999.

Te Kanawa, Kiri, and Michael Foreman. *Land of the Long White Cloud: Maori Myths, Tales, and Legends*. New York, NY: Arcade Publishing, 1989.

Videos

Anyplace Wild: Trekking and Climbing in New Zealand. PBS Home Video, 1998.

New Zealand. Questar Incorporated, 1998.

Websites

<http://maori.culture.co.nz>

<http://www.creativenz.govt.nz/artsnz/maori.html>

<http://www.culture.co.nz>

<http://www.maori.org.nz>

<http://www.maoriart.org.nz>

<http://www.newzealand.com/culture/maori.html>

Organizations

Aotearoa Traditional Maori Performing Arts Society Inc.
P.O. Box 5619
Wellington, New Zealand
Tel: (64) 4-499-6158
Fax: (64) 4-499-6157
E-mail: <admin@atmpas.org.nz>
Website: <http://www.atmpas.org.nz>

The New Zealand Maori Arts and Crafts Institute
PO Box 334, Hemo Road, Rotorua, New Zealand
Tel: (64) 7-348-9047
Fax: (64) 7-348-3418
Website: <http://www.nzmaori.co.nz>

INDEX

ABOUT THE AUTHOR

Steve Theunissen is a freelance writer living
in Masterton, North Island. He was born
and raised in Rotorua and has been a lifelong
student of Maori and Pacific Island culture and
history. His previous works include *The Battle of
the Little Big Horn* and *Through Angel's Eyes*, and
he is a regular contributor to the Uncle John's
Bathroom Reader series. Steve has also written
for print and online publishers in the areas of
American and Polynesian history. Steve would
like to thank his wife Shelley, of the Ngai Te
Rangi Nui Maori tribe, and daughter Chantel
for their support and inspiration throughout
the writing of this book.

PICTURE CREDITS